What to DO
WHEN YOU DON'T KNOW
WHAT to Do

Gilbert Snowden, Jr.

What to Do When You Don't Know What to Do
by Gilbert Snowden, Jr.

Copyright ©1998 Gilbert Snowden, Jr.
All rights reserved. This book is protected under the copyright laws of the United States of America. This book may not be copied or reprinted for commercial gain or profit. The use of short quotations or occasional page copying for personal or group study is permitted and encouraged. Permission will be granted upon request. Unless otherwise identified, Scripture quotations are from the King James Version of the Bible.

ISBN 1-58169-003-7
For Worldwide Distribution
Printed in the U.S.A.

Companion Press
An Imprint of Genesis Communications, Inc.
P.O. Box 91011 • Mobile, AL 36691
888-670-7463
Email: GenesisCom@aol.com

DEDICATION TO MY SON
GILBERT A. SNOWDEN III

I am very proud of you as my son. You gave up family, friends, and familiar territory to venture into unchartered waters with your dad for the cause of Christ. In spite of all the things that you encountered, which I'm sure at times seemed overwhelming and even unbearable, you were able to make it through with the help of the Lord. I thank God for your survival mentality.

God is to be glorified and you are to be commended for a job well done. God truly stood by your side through it all.

My daily prayer for you, son, is that Jesus Christ the righteous Son of God would keep you from the snares of Satan. I decree success, wisdom, and all of God's blessings upon your life.

With love,
Dad

ACKNOWLEDGEMENTS

First and foremost, I want to thank God for standing by my side from the early rocking of the cradle up until this present moment; for without Him, my life would be like a ship without a rudder. Thanks, Jesus.

I am grateful to God for my biological family. Thank you, God, for placing me in the family You have given me. Thank you, my family, for having me. And special thanks to my aunt, Emma Chappell, and her husband, Aaron (now deceased), for all that they did in my life to make its course a little brighter and easier; there is no one quite like the two of you.

This book is also dedicated to all of The Tabernacle of Praise Church family: I truly love you and thank God for you. You have what it takes to make a dream become reality and a vision come to pass. My continual prayer for you is that God would grant each of you your heart's desire, and that you would take the wings of an eagle and fly to your greatest potential. Thank you so much, Tabernacle.

With Much Love,
Pastor Snowden

TABLE OF CONTENTS

1. The Battle Belongs to the Lord..1
2. Only By Prayer and Fasting..14
3. Gather in Unity..26

Chapter One
The Battle Belongs to the Lord

Ye shall not need *to fight in this battle: set yourselves, stand ye* still, *and see the salvation of the Lord with you, O Judah and Jerusalem: fear not, nor be dismayed; tomorrow go out against them: for the Lord will be with you* (II Chronicles 20:17).

Life today involves a continuing sequence of choices that we all must face. We come upon times of trial in our lives where we experience uncertainty as to what we are to do. In II Chronicles 20:1-30, the Word of God tells us that King Jehoshaphat, along with God's people, acted in humility and obedience and obtained the Lord's favor during a crisis. God sovereignly brought about their resounding victory.

The Apple Does Not Fall Far From the Tree

King Jehoshaphat was a mighty leader and one of the best kings in Judah; he was the king of the southern kingdom for 25 years. He was a righteous man, and he attempted to bring about a revival of faith in God among his people. What brought about a revival of faith in God among his people? For one thing, this young king's father, Asa, provided him with a good example that he could emulate. The Bible says that Asa did what was pleasing in the eyes of the Lord (I Kings 15:11). The ability each of us has to affect the lives of others must cause us to be careful how we walk and talk in the world and especially in our homes in front of our children. Children have a tendency to pattern themselves after the example that is set before them—good or bad. You've heard the aphorisms, "like father like son," and "like mother like daughter." More often than we'd like to admit however, mothers do not see eye to eye with their daughters, and fathers with their sons, because we see ourselves and our faults too much in our offspring, and we don't always like what we see.

Look at Jacob: he was a twin, the youngest of the two, and was known to be a deceiver, a conniver, and a supplanter. Where did Jacob get these tendencies? He got them from his mother—she taught him how to be deceptive. Even Jezebel's wicked daughter Athaliah was but a carbon copy of her mother.

We sometimes teach our children how to lie and deceive. For example, if someone calls us on the phone we may tell our children to tell the person that we're not at home; but when they turn around and tell us an untruth, then we're upset. That's wrong when we were the ones who taught them how to lie in the first place!

The ways in which we ourselves face problems during critical and perplexing situations many times will determine how our children will face their problems. If we face our problems with a bottle of pills or alcohol, our children may very well face their problems the same way.

Not by Might, Nor by Power

King Jehoshaphat began his reign by fortifying the cities of

Judah and training an army of more than a million men. On one particular occasion, he received word (II Chronicles 20:2) that he is about to be attacked by the three combined armies of Moab, Ammon, and Mount Seir. The odds were three to one against him. That is how it usually happens to a child of God—the Christian is outnumbered as others team up in opposition. With Gideon, it was something like 500 against one. How did he overcome those odds? What principle determines who wins?

Napoleon said, "That army wins that gets there first with the most," and yet even he met his Waterloo. No student of history would say God is on the side of the largest and most heavily armed battalions. But we are told in Zechariah 4:6 that the greatest victories come about *"by my Spirit, says the Lord."* By doing battle first in the heavenlies through prayer, Samson took the jawbone of an ass and slew 1,000 men with it.

And when he came to Lehi the Philistines shouted against him: and the Spirit of the LORD came mightily upon him, and the cords that were upon his arms became as flax that was burnt with fire, and his bands loosen from off his hands. And Samson said, with the jawbone of an ass, heaps upon heaps, with the jawbone of an ass have I slain a thousand men (Judges 15:14-16).

Romans 8:31 makes it so clear that God is not moved by numbers: *"What shall we then say to these things? If God be for us, who can be against us?"* Who dares to be against you when *God* is on your side?

Fear Not!

II Chronicles 20:3 tells us that King Jehoshaphat, upon

receiving the news that he was about to be attacked by three powerful enemies, became filled with distress and fear. In stressful situations like Jehoshaphat faced, some people feel the need to put on a big front, as though they have no fears, questions, or problems—because of that they are usually the ones who inwardly fight the worst battles. It isn't that you will never feel fear, but the fear you feel should only be momentary.

Fear is not what the Scripture teaches. The phrases "fear not" and "be not afraid" appear at least 100 times in the Bible. Fear is a dangerous human emotion; if left unchecked and unattended to, fear will paralyze and cripple the child of God from doing mighty and great works for the Lord.

There are two kinds of fear: real fear and "shadow fear." Real fear is what you feel if you were to run across an uncaged Alaskan Polar bear. This fear lasts as long as you are in danger, but usually abates when the threat is removed. But if you fear something that does not exist, you are experiencing shadow fear. Continuing to dwell on shadow fears results in maladjusted personalities. This unreal fear is what we must fight, for it attempts to assail us more often than we consciously realize. Therefore, the Bible address 365 "fear nots" to believers—a fresh "fear not" for every day in the year.

God spoke to Abraham and said "fear not" (Genesis 15:1). Moses and the Israelites were encamped at the Red Sea, and Pharaoh and his army approached Israel for their destruction. Through the power of God, Moses told Israel, *"Fear ye not; stand still, and see the salvation of the Lord, which he will shew you to day"* (Exodus 14:13).

The great patriarch David said, *"Though I walk through the valley of the shadow of death, I will fear no evil"* (Psalms 23:4). David was a man who had a great deal of confidence in the God of his salvation. And we are likewise to stand still and see the deliverance God is about to do in our lives, on our behalf. In II Timothy 1:7, the Scripture says: *"For God hath not given us a spirit of fear; but of power and of love and of a sound mind."*

The Bible, which is the infallible, indestructible, imperishable Word of God, clearly informs us that when King Jehoshaphat received word that he was about to be attacked by three united enemies, his heart became filled with distress and fear. Jehoshaphat knew he couldn't possibly stand against such a mighty army, and therefore could not expect to be delivered except by the strong arm of God. Faith overcomes fear, and *God* brings about the victory. But how do we situate ourselves so as to receive the victory God wants to bring about in our lives?

What Must We Do?

These times of trouble arise in all of our lives. How will we respond? In our times of unexpected emergencies, we must also come to some decisions as to what we are to do. At one time or another, all of us face tasks for which we have not been properly equipped, or with decisions we are not ready to make. Humanly speaking, the pressure of life becomes so great at times that we can easily become confused. Have you ever been confused? And if not, just keep on living; confusion you will experience in this life. In Job 14:1, it says, *"Man that is born of a woman is a few days and full of trouble."*

The decision that you and I make in the time of trouble, in the midst of confusion, will have its impact on us for the days to come. How many decisions have we made in the times past, when we were not in Christ, and yet we have not escaped the impact of these decisions: pain, heaviness, and a lack of hope.

The aphorism, "What you don't know can't hurt you," is quite far from the truth. What you don't know can destroy you! Not knowing the consequences and impact of dropping out of school can be just as fatal as not knowing the danger of electricity—both can be disastrous. Not knowing the consequences of substance abuse can ruin or terminate your life.

We have to know the truth, and speak it in love, because the world is not going to prepare you for what is to come. Commercialism tells us how smoothly and refreshingly "Johnny Walker" and "J&B" go down, but it doesn't tell us how roughly they come up! In the book of Hosea, God says His people are destroyed for lack of knowledge—not the heathens but *His people* are destroyed for lack of knowledge of God and His ways. We must strive to get the knowledge of God from His Word and apply it to our lives. We must use every means at our disposal to build up the kingdom of God.

Seek the Lord Through Prayer

In his sudden and dangerous emergency, Jehoshaphat concluded that he needed to do three things with the cooperation of his people (II Chronicles 20:3-4). The first thing King Jehoshaphat decided to do was to set himself to seek the Lord (v.3). He began to call on the Lord with all his might. As we face a problem, our first response should be to seek the Lord through prayer. Prayer is the highest activity of the soul.

Prayer is our communication system with God. It is still the fastest system there is today. You can write a letter or go see someone, use the telephone, send a telegram, fax or e-mail; but nothing is faster or more effective than prayer. The earth is 93 million miles from the sun, and the sun's rays travel for eight minutes and 20 seconds to reach the earth, but did you know that prayer reaches our heavenly Father even quicker than that? Throughout the Scriptures you can find where the patriarchs prayed, and God heard and answered their prayer. He may not answer when we think He should, but He's always right on time. He moves in His own way and in His own time. We are not on our own time, but are on God's perfect time.

Seeking the Lord should be a priority in each of our lives. The Bible says we ought to always pray and never faint or lose heart. But what is prayer, and what does it involve?

Talking to God

Prayer is our talking to God. In II Samuel 5:19-25, we have a good example of one of God's servants talking to Him. In this passage, David, the man after God's own heart, has been anointed to be king over Israel. But when the Philistines heard that he had been anointed king *over all Israel,* they came up to seek David. It must first be understood that the Philistines were enemies of the people of God since the time of Moses up until David. As long as David was only ruling over Judah or the cities of Judah, the Philistines had no problem with him. But when he had control over the whole country, he started encountering difficulties with them.

The enemy will usually attack when he sees you begin to rule more effectively in God's kingdom. As you more fully experience God's purpose and plan for your life and begin to positively affect other people's lives, the destroyer will come against you with much greater intensity.

The Philistines came up against David to try to wipe him out, attempting to stop him before he could get himself established. But the Bible says that David found out the Philistines' plans concerning him. In verse 19, it is written:

And David inquired of the Lord saying, shall I go up to the Philistines? Wilt thou deliver them into my hand? And the Lord said unto David, Go up: for I will doubtless deliver the Philistines unto thy hand.

In this passage, David is talking to God about his situation. The Scripture tells us to make our request known to God, for He hears and answers prayer. David needed direction concerning this situation, so he called on the God of his salvation. We have always been told that we shouldn't question God, but how are we to know what to do in some delicate situations if we do not ask our heavenly Father? We aren't to doubt God, but to ask what He wants for us; and in order to do so, there has to be a channel of communication open between God and us.

With people you love, you make it your business to ask them what they mean, so that you understand them and they you—this is what prayer is all about! We tell God of our inability to save ourselves and that we absolutely need His strength, direction, and provision for everything. In order to have God listen to us, to hear our prayers, we must get used to saying to Him, "Speak, Lord; your servant is listening" (I Samuel 3:9).

Listening to God

In addition to our speaking to God, we must listen for *His response* in this loving dialogue or two-way street of communication. Prayer is not solely about our talking, as in a monologue, but it also involves our listening to Him: *"Faith cometh by hearing"* (Romans 10:17). In II Samuel 5:19-23 we find David talking to God, but we also find God coming back to David, telling him what to do about the situation he's in. If we are going to receive instructions and directions, then there will come a time when we must listen. Sometimes as soon we've finished talking to God, we're up and on our way. That's not good, because we haven't given Him a chance to talk to us, and He has more to say than we ever could.

David spent time talking to God, but he spent even more time listening. The Lord told David to go up against the Philistines because that He would deliver the enemy into his hands. David did exactly as he was instructed, and the enemy was defeated. But the conflict didn't stop there; the enemy rose up again against David. What did David do then? He inquired of the Lord again. Never take God for granted, and never feel as though you know how, or in what way, God will work out a situation for you.

When the Philistines came up against him this time, David wasn't so overconfident that he thought he knew the mind of God and didn't need to pray to Him. The Scripture says to pray without ceasing. So David called on God a second time, and the Lord told him to go behind the mulberry trees and listen to the sound of marching in the air upon the top of the tree. Then God said, "That's your signal that I've gone out before you." David listened a second time, followed through with God's instructions, and received the victory. So once again the key to David's victory was to listen and obey the instructions of the Lord.

The Bible tells us in James 1:22: *"But be ye doers of the Word, and not hearers only, deceiving your own selves."* There is power in listening to the voice of God, because He'll lead you out on top every time.

In Exodus 15, just after Moses and the Israelites marched through the parted waters of the Red Sea, they arrived at the bitter waters of Marah. The water was too bitter to drink, and the people began to murmur against Moses, saying "What shall we drink?" Moses then cried out to God. The Lord directed Moses to a tree, by which, when he cast it into the waters, the waters were made sweet. Moses followed through with what the Lord told him to do in faith and obedience. Moses said that if the people would diligently hearken unto the voice of the Lord and do what is right in his sight, heeding His commandments and keeping all His statutes, God would not allow them to suffer from any of the diseases He had brought upon the Egyptians. For God said, *"I am the Lord that healeth thee."* But we have to cooperate with Him in order for Him to heal us, and listening has a very important part in allowing God's work to be done in us.

Thinking With God

Prayer is our thinking with God. Philippians 2:5 says, *"Let this mind be in you which was also in Christ Jesus."* When God formed man from the dust of the earth, the Scripture tells us that He breathed into man's nostrils the breath of life, and man became a living soul (Genesis 2:7). Not only did He breathe into man's nostrils, but He also equipped man with a very powerful and wonderful mechanism that we call the human mind.

The mind is the control center of life; it has been compared to a computer. Mechanically speaking this is a good comparison—both the mind and the computer are switching networks that have multiple interconnections. Both instruments store, retrieve, and dispatch information and messages which can determine actions elsewhere. Proverbs 23:7 tells us, *"For as he thinketh in his heart so is he."* Since everything starts in our head or in our thought-life, Philippians 2:5 challenges us to *"Let this mind be in you which was also in Christ."* The only way the mind of Christ can reside in us is when we let the Word of Christ dwell richly in us by actively studying it.

What does the mind of Christ really consist of? We know that the mind leads to acts. During His earthly ministry, Jesus Christ had a mind of compassion that inspired acts of love and mercy. If we are to be followers of Christ with His mind, we too must have a mind and heart of compassion for our brothers and sisters in the Body of Christ, as well as for those who are presently outside the Body.

Compassion goes farther than mere kindness. Ephesians 4:32 says to *"be ye kind, tenderhearted, forgiving one to another."* Jesus *always* showed acts of compassion. Matthew 14:14 says Jesus *"went forth, and saw a great multitude, and was moved to compassion towards them."* We too ought to be moved with compassion, if the mind of Christ is dwelling in us.

There should also be a humbleness in our thought. In Philippians 2:8, the Bible says of Jesus, *"And being found in fashion as a man, he humbled himself, and became obedient unto death, even the death of the cross."* Humility rules out striving in thought or deed on our own strength, outside of obedience to the Lord:

> *For the weapons of our warfare are not carnal, but mighty through God to the pulling down of strong holds; casting down imaginations, and every high thing that exalteth itself against the knowledge of God, and bringing into captivity every thought to the obedience of Christ* (II Corinthians 10:4-5).

In John 20:21, Jesus says, *"Peace be unto you: as my Father hath sent me, even so I send you."* But how are we to think, act, and witness in peace?

The servant of the Lord must not strive but be gentle unto all men, apt to teach, patient, in meekness instructing . . . that they may recover themselves out of the snare of the devil, who are taken captive by him at his will (II Timothy 2:24-26).

When we get what we want by striving, it has cost too much—let Christ do the job through you. As you pray, thinking in union with God's mind, allow His mind to form yours, so that it might take on His compassionate image and likeness, and others' lives will be touched by your love.

Submitting to God

Prayer is our submitting to God. James 4:7 says, *"Submit yourself therefore to God. Resist the devil, and he will flee from you."* To submit means to allow oneself to be subjected; to yield. To submit to God's instructions is probably one of the most difficult tasks for the believer. In II Samuel 5, King David submitted to God's instructions regarding whether He should go up against the enemy, or keep still. God instructed David to go up against the enemy, and he received victory. The second time, God gave him different instructions, and because David again submitted to the Lord, the enemy was overtaken. The victory was won because of David's submission to God's instructions, or obedience, which Scripture tells us is better than sacrifice.

In every aspect of our lives, be it our walk with the Lord, our marriage, our job, etc., the choice is ours: obey God and be blessed, or disobey Him and be cursed. The more we obey, the more we will be blessed; the less we do, the less God can bless us, if at all.

Living and Working in the Presence of God

Since our goal is to have our lives blessed by God, prayer is our first avenue to get there. Prayer is our living and working in the presence of the Lord. In Psalms 16:11, it is written, *"Thou wilt shew me the path of life: in your presence is fullness of joy; at thy right hand there are pleasures for evermore."* Living and working "in the presence" can only happen as we commune with Him. If we draw near to God, He will draw nigh unto us. When we have our quiet time with the Lord Jesus Christ, He will show up, and we will experience His presence.

But our God is a jealous God, tolerating no rivals (Deuteronomy 5:6-7). We need to shut out every voice that distracts us from His own—cutting off the TV, and sometimes not answering the phone for a period of time, so we can get into the Word of God. For in the Word of God we find the source of joy and contentment in our lives. Many Christians today seem not to have any joy, but if they would use the Word to get into His presence, that unspeakable joy would come rushing into their spirit. All the work of the Lord that's done, which we are privileged to do, is only being done because on a daily basis we are learning how to live and work in His presence. With Him being a holy and perfect God and us imperfect people, that's a privilege. If you never have thought about that, try meditating on it for awhile. The Holy Spirit can speak to you and reveal to you more fully how great a privilege it is to live in God's presence.

Chapter Two
Only By Prayer and Fasting

How to Overcome Great Odds

There is no way that you or I can walk with God and *not* expect to have some form of confrontation with the enemy, so we ought to be prepared. Adversity is a season of unusual attack, so we ought to consider using unusual weapons. Fasting is a feared weapon in spiritual battle. The more we fast and pray, the more we will experience God's presence and gain direction for our lives, and hence the more the enemy will try to oppose us. The greater the opposition, the greater the blessing we will receive from our Lord, who will entrust us with increased responsibilities.

Fasting, for example, was used by God's people in the scene we have mentioned in the first chapter where the Israelites were being confronted with possible destruction by the people of Ammon, Moab, and Mount Seir (II Chronicles 20:10). Thank God that Jehoshaphat and his people were loved and cared for by God Almighty.

In this life, many times it may seem as though you may be outnumbered, but the Word of God says that "if God be for you, who can be against you?" But if God be against you, it does not matter how many may be for you.

The *Holman Bible Dictionary* defines the word *fasting* as "refraining from eating food." Fasting does involve limiting our food intake, among other things. In Esther 4:16 the Word says, *"and ye fast for me, and neither eat nor drink three days, night or day."* Esther was a woman who was confronted with the possible slaughter of her people. She depended on the weapon of fasting to accomplish her goal of helping to save them.

Fasting will bring the miraculous presence of the Lord into a situation for the benefit of His people. As the people of God, we too should realize the power of fasting, for, as the slogan goes, "If you fast, you will last." We can accomplish our desired ends by adding to our arsenals the potent weapon of fasting.

In Matthew 4:2, when Jesus had fasted 40 days and 40 nights, the Scripture says He was hungry afterwards. Jesus Christ, the Son of the living God, fasted for what would seem like an eternity to us—if *He* fasted, then what about us? But it is very important to be led by the Holy Spirit when we fast. The Bible does not say that He did not drink any water; it simply says He fasted and afterwards hungered.

A Life-changing Encounter

In Acts 9:9, the apostle Paul fasted three days, foregoing food and drink. Those who are familiar with Paul know that he was a prolific contributor to the New Testament; he was responsible for about two-thirds of the writings contained therein. Prior to his conversion, Paul was an aggressive persecutor of the Christian faith; he certainly lacked the Lord's mind and heart of compassion. One day, while on his way down to the Damascus Synagogue to do harm to some Christians, he was met by the Lord Jesus Christ and thrown from his beast (Acts 9:3-4). At this point, you could say that he had a significant encounter with the Lord (vs.4-6).

Whenever you have an encounter with the Lord, some changes are going to take place. Paul went for three days and nights without sight and without food, in the meantime no doubt receiving his spiritual vision and satisfying his tremendous spiritual hunger. He eventually received his physical sight back after the laying on of hands by the disciple Ananias.

Fasting can provide an eye-opening experience in our lives too. Have you ever tried fasting for three days and nights? If not, ask for God's direction and watch and see how God *will* move on your behalf. Our God is an awesome God, and when He moves or speaks, everything has to come to a standstill, because He is God.

Focus on God

And Jehoshaphat feared and set himself to seek the Lord and proclaimed a fast through Judah (II Chronicles 20:3).

King Jehoshaphat called for a fast. He sounded the alarm, making it known that it was time for a group fast. Sometimes God will reveal through His leader that it's time for a *corporate fast*—time for all of the assembly to come together for fasting purposes. For if we're to see changes, if strongholds are to be brought down, and chains are to fall from God's people, then God's people must go on a fast.

More than just abstaining from food, fasting involves

focus. When fasting, we should put our focus on God. Fasting for a spiritual purpose causes us to be more sensitive to the Spirit of God. God is also pleased by our effort to deny ourselves for the sake of the kingdom, and so He bestows the grace on us that we need to faithfully serve Him. Therefore, the combination of fasting and seeking the Lord intensifies our experience of the Lord's presence.

Maintaining our focus is very important while fasting. If we stay focused on God while we're fasting, we can be assured that God will move on our behalf. You see, *broken focus* is the goal of all satanic attack. If the enemy can convince us to trust in ourselves to the exclusion of God, we're in his domain.

However, there is a proper way to focus on ourselves. If our first and foremost focus is on God, who takes care of our circumstances, we should also have time to focus on ourself, as we humble ourselves so that God might be glorified in our bodies. Psalms 35:3 says, *"I humbled my soul with fasting."* This very important statement came from David during a critical time in his life. David knew about the power of fasting, and what it could do in the life of a child of God.

All through the Psalms, David gives this testimony. In Psalms 69:10 he says, *"When I wept* and chastened *my soul with fasting,"* David received some priceless spiritual benefits from God. In I Corinthians 6:20, Paul says *"for ye are bought with a price: therefore glorify God in your body, and in your spirit, which are God's."* So remember: when we are fasting, God is being glorified in our bodies. How is God being glorified? Due to the fact that the Holy Spirit lives in you and is having His way in you, and many strongholds and bondages are being shaken from your life while you are fasting, God is being glorified as others see His power at work in your life!

Focus on a Particular Situation

While fasting, we must also focus on a *particular situation*. King Jehoshaphat had his focus on a particular situation, and so he proclaimed a fast to ask the help of the Lord (II Chronicles 20:3). God honors a fast if it is done to honor Him. It is comforting to know that we can receive the help of the Lord in our day of trouble or just in our day-to-day affairs. Sometimes we may ask the help of our friends and family, but they may be unable to help us. However, no matter what the problem, God can help us. There is no problem that God cannot solve, no question he cannot answer. Try Him and see.

He Supplies All Our Needs

Then I proclaimed a fast there to to seek of him a right way for us and our little ones, and for all our substance (Ezra 8:21-23).

Through fasting, you can get directions from God concerning a situation. You will become more sensitive to the Spirit of God and come to clearly know what God wants you to do in a given situation. Our Father who is in heaven wants us to seek Him for guidance in our daily affairs. We don't always know which road to take or which way to go, but if we seek Him, He will guide us to where we are meant to be.

Even when it comes down to our sustenance, fasting unto the Lord causes Him to move on our behalf and to supply our need, not solely according to the need but according to His abundance. Philippians 4:19 makes this point when it says, *"But my God shall supply all your need according to His riches in glory by Christ Jesus."* Whatever you need, God's got it; and if God doesn't have it, then it means you and I don't need it, because He has everything that is good, true, and worthwhile.

Let Your Fasts Be Worshipful

As they ministered unto the Lord and fasted, the Holy Spirit said separate me Barnabas and Saul for the work whereunto I have called them. And when they had fasted and prayed, and laid their hands on them, they sent them away (Acts 13:2-3).

Worship must be a priority in the life of every Christian, especially during times of fasting. Fasting is also a worship experience, a ministry unto the Lord. It is not enough to say you are fasting—prayer, worship, and extending God's love and mercy to others are essential for your fast to please God.

Fast in Faith

God will restore what the locust has eaten when fasting is involved (Joel 2:15-27). Fasting can even fix our shortcomings, such as unbelief and lack of trust in God, which can hold us back. The boy mentioned in Matthew 17:14-15 was a lunatic; he was being vexed by the devil, and his father brought him to the disciples of Christ to cure him, but they were unable to help. Jesus rebuked the devil, and it departed from the boy on the spot. After the child was cured, the disciples asked Jesus why they were unable to cast out the devil.

He told them:

For if you have faith as a grain of mustard seed, ye shall say unto this mountain, Remove hence to yonder place; and it shall remove; and nothing shall be impossible unto you. Howbeit this kind goeth not out but by prayer and fasting. (Matthew 17:20-21).

Many habitual miscues that persist in plaguing our lives can only be conquered by the power of fasting with unwavering faith. Even when there is unbelief in our lives, through prayer and fasting, this spirit can be removed. There is no mountain that will be able to stand in our way if we would take up the weapon used so effectively throughout the Scriptures. As the Spirit leads you to fast, there are several different types of fasts to choose from, according to *God's Guide to Fasting*, by Jersey Charles.

Types of Fasts

A. **Partial or restricted fasts** (some food is eaten)

1. *"Prove thy servants, I beseech thee, ten days; and let them give us pulse to eat and water to drink"* (Daniel 1:12).

2. *"I ate no pleasant bread, neither came flesh nor wine in my mouth"* (Daniel 10:3).

3. *"And his* [John the Baptist's] *meat was locusts and wild honey"* (Matthew 3:4).

4. *"And he* [John the Baptist] *shall drink neither wine nor strong drink"* (Luke 1:15).

B. **Natural fasts** (only water is taken)

1. *"And when he had fasted 40 days and 40 nights, he was afterward anhungered"* [not thirsty] (Matthew 4:2).

2. *"Paul besought them to take meat, saying, This day is the 14th day that ye have tarried and continued fasting, having taken nothing"* (Acts 27:33).

C. **Total fasts** (no food or water)
1. "[for one night] *Ezra did eat no bread nor drink water* (Ezra 10:6).
2. *"And fast ye for me* [Queen Esther] *and neither eat nor drink three days, night or day"* (Esther 4:16).
3. "[For three days and nights] *and he* [Paul] *was three days without sight, and neither did eat nor drink"* (Acts 9:9).

D. **Supernatural fasts** (No food or water taken for a lengthy period; must be entered only at the Lord's specific calling)
1. *"Then I* [Moses] *abode in the mount 40 days and 40 nights; I neither did eat bread nor drink water"* (Deuteronomy 9:9).
2. *"And he* [Elijah] *arose, and did eat and drink, and went in the strength of that meat 40 days and 40 nights unto Horeb, the mount of God"* (I Kings 19:8).

Classification of Fasts

A. **Private fasts**
   1. Deuteronomy 9:9
   2. Deuteronomy 9:18
   3. Daniel 10:2-3
   4. Isaiah 37:1
   5. Matthew 4:1-12
   6. Matthew 6:18

B. **Public fasts**

1. Judges 20:26
2. Esther 4:2

C. National fasts
1. I Chronicles 20:3
2. Nehemiah 9:1
3. Esther 4:16
4. Jonah 3:5-8

D. Congregational fasts
1. Jeremiah 36:6
2. Joel 1:1-14; 2:15
3. Acts 13:1-3; 14:23

E. Religious fasts
1. Leviticus 16:29-31
2. Numbers 6:3
3. Judges 13:5
4. Acts 27:9

F. Special fasts
1. Matthew 9:14-15
2. Acts 27:33
3. I Corinthians 7:5

G. Marital fasts
1. II Samuel 11:11
2. I Corinthians 7:5

H. Voluntary fasts
1. Matthew 6:16-18
2. Matthew 9:14-15
3. Luke 18:12

4. Acts 10:30
5. Acts 13:2-3

I. **Involuntary fasts**
1. I Samuel 1:7-8
2. I Samuel 20:34
3. I Samuel 28:20
4. I Samuel 28:22-23
5. II Samuel 1:11-12
6. II Samuel 3:33-35
7. I Kings 21:4-5
8. I Kings 25:32
9. I Chronicles 10:12
10. Job 33:19-20
11. Psalms 42:3
12. Psalms 102:42

J. **False fasts** (things not to do when fasting)
1. Fast as the hypocrites
2. Be sanctimonious
3. Fast unto men
4. Reveal the fact that you are fasting
5. Disfigure your face (Matthew 6:16-18)
6. Fast when it's too late (II Samuel 12:22-23; Jeremiah 14:11-12)
7. Have a wrong nature or attitude (Acts 23:1)
8. Don't fast to:
    (a) Afflict the soul to attract God (Isaiah 58:3)
    (b) Oppress your employees (Isaiah 58:3)
    (c) Stir up strife and contention (Isaiah 58:4)
    (d) Be cruel to others (Isaiah 58:4)

What to Do When You Don't Know What to Do

Fasting does not change God; He is the same before, during, and after your fast. Fasting will change *you and me*, helping us become more sensitive to the Spirit of God. Fasting has a way of causing an outpouring of the Holy Spirit in our lives:

> *Blow the trumpet in Zion; sanctify a fast; call a solemn assembly . . . And it shall come to pass afterward, that I will pour out my spirit upon all flesh . . . And I will shew wonders in the heavens and in the earth* (Joel 2:15,28,30).

So when you fast, the power of the Holy Spirit is manifested in a special way, causing great things to happen. Remember, while Paul was on the road to Damascus, he was visited powerfully by the risen Lord Jesus. As a result of this encounter, Paul lost his sight, or the limited vision he had had of how to live his life. Blind for three days—the time our Lord was in the tomb—Paul experienced the life-changing power of God, and he came to *life*. He could see as he had never been able to do before! What enhanced his spiritual transformation was his fasting that helped him focus on God and find out what God had for him. He then received a great blessing from God—his sight—and fulfill all that God had for him to do.

You and I may fast and receive our sight, too, in the areas of our lives where there may be blindness. Even today fasting is a very powerful weapon, one that God's people ought to take advantage of. If you've never fasted before, seek the Lord and get His guidance as to how He would have you fast, and see if a change doesn't take place in your daily walk with the Master.

From personal experience, I've seen the power of God and an outpouring of grace take place because of fasting. Don't think that this is something to do just to pass the time away; fasting is done to bring the manifestation and outpouring of the Holy Spirit into your life and particular circumstance.

Look at what happened when Jehoshaphat and all his people fasted: their cry went up before God, who hears and answers prayers, especially when a sacrifice is made. As one songwriter put it, "Turn your plates down, fast and pray; Jesus will always bring you out." Try it and see what the Master can and will do on your behalf.

Chapter Three
Gather in Unity

Unity and Uniformity

The third thing King Jehoshaphat concluded to do was to hold a national convention at Jerusalem (II Chronicles 20:4-5). The Word of God informs us that this good king called for a convention so that God's people could get together for the sole purpose of seeking or calling on God. The people assembled out of the cities of Judah to attend this gathering. The wives and the children, including the infants, came (v.13); everyone took part in this great event. What is so interesting is that, when they assembled themselves, they did not do so just anywhere, but went into the House of the Lord. Not only did they meet in the House of God, but they were all with one accord. Where there is unity, you will find strength. Psalms 133 says:

> *Behold how good and pleasant it is for brethren to dwell together in unity. It is like the precious ointment upon the head, that ran down the beard, even Aaron's beard: that went down the skirts of his garments; as the dew of Hermon, and as the dew that descended upon the mountains of Zion: for there the LORD commanded the blessing even life for evermore.*

Gather in Unity

We do find much *uniformity* in the Church—we're dressed up alike from the top of our heads to the bottom of our feet—but we don't have any real *unity,* and disunity is dangerous. However, when two or more Christians stick together, they can light up an entire city with the light of Christ. Unity is essential for the Gospel to be spread effectively.

There is much power in forces that unite together. Look in the animal kingdom: animals travel in numbers for strength and protection. When the zebra, for instance, travels alone or is by itself, it is an easy prey for a lion. But if the zebra travels in numbers and is attacked by a lion, they flee, their stripes serving as an illusion that confuses the lion. The lion is unable to detect which zebra is which, or where one ends and another begins; and the zebras do not die but live. If we would enter into the depths of the sea, we would also notice how fish travel in large numbers, or schools, for protection. If the animal kingdom and sea world are supported and protected in numbers, shouldn't we stick together for our own good?

Abraham Lincoln, the 16th President of the United States, quoted the Scriptures in his acceptance speech on June 17, 1858, pointing out that a house divided against itself cannot stand (Matthew 12:25). Lincoln was simply informing us of the effects of division. In 1971, Tony Hiller and Peter Simon composed a song entitled, "United We Stand; Divided We Fall," which speaks of unity and division. Should it surprise us that the strategy of the enemy of our souls is to divide us and thereby conquer us?

The way to combat division is to be united in Christ. Jesus once said in Matthew 18:20, *"For where two or more are gathered in My name, there I am in the midst."* The power of unity and agreement is that Christ's presence is brought quite powerfully among us. The secret of the blessing of the early Church may be summed up in one word: unity. The hearts of the first disciples beat as one in their love for God and each other. All through the Word of God, and especially in the book of Acts, the words "one accord" occur again and again. The Word says "accord," not "discord." Amos 3:3 asks, *"Can two walk together except that they be agreed?"* There has to be unity between people before they will be able to walk together. How can you possibly walk together for really meaningful purposes without unity? When there is lack of unity you will find the enemy creating havoc amongst the people, and our God is not the author of confusion but of peace.

The Power of the Prayer of Agreement

In Daniel 2:1-10 we see that in the second year of King Nebuchadnezzar's reign, he had a terrifying nightmare and awoke trembling with fear. To make matters worse, he couldn't remember his dream! He immediately called in all his magicians, incantationists, sorcerers, and astrologers and demanded that they tell him what his dream had been. "I've had a terrible nightmare," he said as they stood before him, "and I can't remember what it was. Tell me, for I fear some tragedy awaits me." The astrologers, speaking in Aramaic, then said to him, "Sir, tell us the dream, and then we can tell you what it means." But the King replied, "I tell you the dream is gone; I can't remember it. And if you won't tell me what it was and what it means, I'll have you torn limb from limb and your houses made into heaps of rubble."

Nebuchadnezzar was one of the meanest men recorded in biblical history. At the age of 18, he conquered Nineveh; at 25 he was world ruler. He was narcissistic and egomaniacal; he was completely controlled by his pride. For example, when Nebuchadnezzar seized Jerusalem, he chopped off the necks of the sons of Zedekiah, gouging out Zedekiah's eyes so that the last thing the father saw was his sons losing their necks. Then history says he took Zedekiah's tongue out of his mouth and nailed it to his chin so he wouldn't hear him whimpering as he marched him across the desert with Daniel, Hananiah, Mishael, and Azariah (Shadrach, Meshach and Abednego).

But now the King was furious that he could not remember what he had dreamt, and even more so that his "wise men" could not interpret what he could not tell them! Therefore he came to the conclusion that he would destroy all who were considered wise men in his territory, including Daniel, Shadrach, Meshach, and Abednego, who were living in Babylon at the time.

Then Daniel went in and asked the King to give him time, and he would show him the interpretation. Daniel went to his house and made the problem known to his companions, Hananiah, Mishael, and Azariah (Daniel 2:16-17). They asked the God of heaven to show them His mercy by telling them the secret, so that they would not die with the others. That night in a vision, God told Daniel what the King had dreamt. There is great power in people uniting together, especially in prayer, to change things.

Where there is no prayer, there is no power; where there is little prayer, there is little power; and where there is much prayer, there is much power. In every situation of life we ought to utter a word of prayer to our Father God. An increase in power begins when two or more are gathered in unity. Jesus promises us tremendous results from the prayer of agreement. In Matthew 18:19, Jesus said:

Again I say unto you that if two of you shall agree on earth as touching anything that they shall ask, it shall be done for them of my Father which is in heaven.

King Jehoshaphat and all those who came from Judah on his behalf assembled in the posture of prayer, the prayer of agreement. They were all crying out to God concerning the same situation, the same problem. Isn't it wonderful when you can find a group of people who will come together for the one purpose of seeking to resolve a problem? While Jehoshaphat was speaking to the Lord, God heard him and sent him the answer to their dilemma through Jahaziel (II Chronicles 20:14-17). It is wonderful to know that, whether we are at a conference or a convention, a women's or men's fellowship, God will hear and answer our prayers. His answer may not come when we want it to come, but God is always on time for His purpose to be accomplished.

He Often Uses Others to Answer Our Prayers

God sent the answer through Jahaziel, whose name means, "God seeth" or "God reveals." Yes, our God knows and sees all. The Bible informs us that the eyes of the Lord are always upon His children; His eyes are always upon the righteous ones. God is not just simply good; He is much better than that, but we can't find one single word that will fully describe His awesomeness. He does all things well, far above anything we could imagine. He knows exactly what to do, when to do it, and who to use to do it. It is not always the one we think He will use to get the job done; He often uses the most unlikely of candidates. God doesn't call the qualified; He qualifies those whom He calls.

Gather in Unity

One thing we love about God is that He gets other folks involved in our situation. For you see, no man is an island. We can't live for ourselves and by ourselves; we need one another on this Christian journey. In II Kings 4, we see a prime example of God getting folks involved in another's situation. The Bible tells us there was a widow that Elisha provided oil for. She came to tell Elisha of her husband's death, a man who loved God. But her husband owed some money when he died, and now the creditor was demanding it back. If she didn't pay it back, the creditor told her he would take her two sons as his slaves. (Poor people during these times were allowed to pay their debts by selling themselves or their children as slaves.) Elisha asked the widow how much food she had in the house. She replied that they had nothing except a jar of olive oil. (Even when you think you don't have anything, there's always something in the house.)

Once the prophet found out she had some olive oil, he instructed her to borrow pots and pans from all her friends and neighbors. Then he told her to go into the house with her sons and shut the door behind herself. She was then told to pour oil from her jar into the pots and pans, setting them aside when they were filled. When they were all filled, the oil stopped flowing. When she told the prophet what happened, he told her to go and sell the oil to pay her debt, with enough left over for her and her sons to live on. God is our Provider. He also has a way of getting other people involved in our situation who will be able to help us in more than one way.

Faithful Spirits and Unfaithful Ones

Now there are some people who will get themselves

involved in your situation to no good end. Many times they want to find out what motivates you, what makes you tick. They find out about your business on the north side of town, and by the time you get home your business has been told all over the south side of town. But when we tell something to our God, He spreads our business all around town to those who will bring help. In Proverbs 11:13, *"talebearer revealeth secrets; but he that is of a faithful spirit concealeth the matter."* In other words, Solomon, the writer of Proverbs, is saying that a person who has a loose tongue will reveal secrets, but a person of a faithful spirit will keep what is told to them in confidence. God bless the person of a faithful spirit! Many a soul has been wounded, pierced, and almost destroyed because of the unfaithfulness of someone who couldn't keep what was told them in private.

Keep to yourself what is said in private because you never know when you may have to share some of the deep things concerning your own life. Treat others as you would have them treat you; love your neighbor as you would like to be loved.

Trust God with Your Life

The decisions that we make and the actions we take in the time of crisis can determine how we will be situated with regards to tomorrow. How often we look back on decisions we made in the past. We can feel the effects of those decisions today, whether good or bad.

Asa was the father of King Jehoshaphat. In the 39th year of his reign, Asa became seriously ill with gout—a disease of the feet (I Kings 15:23). Gout causes all the uric acids to settle in the connecting tissues of the feet, causing excruciating pain.

Instead of looking to *Jehovah Rapha,* "the Lord who healeth thee," Asa put his trust solely in the doctors, and he died. Asa trusted God to help him win battles, but he didn't trust Him enough to heal him.

The doctors can cut you open from the crown of your head to the souls of your feet, but if God isn't also involved with the healing, their work is just like putting a drop in a bucket or rolling water off the back of a duck. Healing either will not occur, or so very little will happen that it won't make a difference in your condition. But when we look at Jehoshaphat, we see that during the time of trouble he put his trust and confidence in the God of the universe. In Psalms 20:7 the psalmist says, *"Some trust in chariots, and some in horses: but we will remember the name of the Lord our God."* King Jehoshaphat remembered the name of his God and put his trust in Him.

Upon putting his trust in God, he was able to receive a tremendous victory over the enemy; God brought quick deliverance. God can deliver quickly, or He may decide to deliver later, but deliver He will. Just as King Jehoshaphat trusted, you too can put your trust in the God of this universe and watch Him move on your behalf. In Isaiah 54:17, the prophet says:

No weapon that is formed against thee shall prosper, and every tongue that shall rise against thee in judgement thou shalt condemn. This is the heritage of the servants of the Lord and their righteousness is of me, saith the Lord.

No matter what the enemy of our God attempts, we need to tell him, "It won't work, so just drop your weapon and move from me, because I'm a winner in Christ."

What to Do When You Don't Know What to Do

So when you don't know what to do, let's do as King Jehoshaphat did: first, he set himself to seek the Lord; second, he called for a national fast; and third, he held a national convention at Jerusalem. Seek the Lord by prayer and fasting in union with the people of God, and trust Him to provide for all your needs, even that of your very life.

And on the fourth day they assembled themselves in the valley of Berachah; for there they blessed the LORD: therefore the name of the same place was called, the valley of Berachah, unto this day. Then they returned, every man of Judah and Jerusalem, and Jehoshaphat in the forefront of them, to go again to Jerusalem with joy; for the LORD had made them to rejoice over their enemies. And they came to Jerusalem with psalteries and harps and trumpets unto the house of the LORD. And the fear of God was on all the kingdoms of those countries, when they had heard that the LORD fought against the enemies of Israel. So the realm of Jehoshaphat was quiet; for his God gave him rest round about (II Chronicles 20: 26-30).